Three Days in the Country

Patrick Marber was born in 1964. He lives in London with his wife and their three sons.

Ivan Turgenev was born in Orel in central Russia in 1818. He studied at the universities in Moscow, St Petersburg and Berlin and worked briefly for the civil service before turning to writing. *A Month in the Country* was published in 1855, but not staged until 1872. As well as other plays and short stories, he wrote several novels, including *Fathers and Sons*, which examined the social, political and philosophical issues of the time. Living mainly in Baden-Baden and Paris, he was acquainted with a number of influential writers and met Dickens and Trollope among others on his travels to England. Turgenev was widely perceived to be the first major Russian writer to achieve great success in Europe. He died in Paris in 1883.

Arkady

PATRICK MARBER

Three Days in the Country

A version of Turgenev's
A Month in the Country

FABER & FABER

First published in 2015
by Faber and Faber Ltd
Bloomsbury House, 74–77 Great Russell Street,
London WC1B 3DA

Reprinted with minor revisions September 2015

Typeset by Country Setting, Kingsdown, Kent CT14 8ES
Printed in England by CPI Group (UK) Ltd, Croydon CR0 4YY

A CIP record for this book
is available from the British Library

978-0-571-32770-6

FSC
www.fsc.org
MIX
Paper from
responsible sources
FSC® C013604

This play is dedicated to Ian Rickson

Acknowledgements

My grateful thanks to Sonia Friedman who commissioned this play. It was her idea that I should do a version of *A Month in the Country*, and her enthusiasm and encouragement have been invaluable.

I worked from a literal translation by Patrick Miles who gave me numerous notes on the original, alerted me to details I'd missed and was a fantastic source of wisdom and humour throughout the writing and rehearsing of the play.

Ian Rickson read every draft, advised, counselled and radically improved the thing throughout its period of composition. It was the first play I'd written for seven years and I couldn't have done it without him.

The original company of actors at the National Theatre were a pleasure to work with. Their great spirit and brilliance here acknowledged.

Finally, Turgenev. He said, modestly, that his play was way too long and undeserving of performance. *A Month in the Country* is rarely performed in its entirety (it would take well over four hours) and has been reconceived and 'versioned' throughout its long life. I adored being in Turgenev's world and responding to it with this shorter – at times faithful at other times unfaithful – account of my time there.

PM, June 2015

Three Days in the Country was first presented in the Lyttelton auditorium of the National Theatre, London, on 21 July 2015. The cast was as follows:

Arkady John Light
Natalya Amanda Drew
Kolya Tom Burgering /
  Joshua Gringras / Joel Thomas
Vera Lily Sacofsky
Anna Lynn Farleigh
Lizaveta Debra Gillett
Rakitin John Simm
Schaaf Gawn Grainger
Belyaev Royce Pierreson
Shpigelsky Mark Gatiss
Bolshintsov Nigel Betts
Matvey Nicholas Bishop
Katya Cherrelle Skeete

Ensemble Paige Carter, Mark Extance,
  Matthew Lloyd Davies, Mateo Oxley,
  Cassie Raine, Lisa Tramontin

Director Patrick Marber
Designer Mark Thompson
Lighting Neil Austin
Music and Sound Adam Cork
Movement Polly Bennett
Music Director Sam Cable

Stage Manager David Marsland
Deputy Stage Manager Fiona Bardsley
Assistant Stage Manager Polly Rowe
Staff Director Daniel Raggett

Characters

Arkady
a rich landowner, forties

Natalya
his wife

Kolya
their son, ten

Vera
their ward, seventeen

Anna
Arkady's mother, sixties

Lizaveta
Anna's companion, around fifty

Rakitin
a friend of the family, forties

Schaaf
a German tutor

Belyaev
Kolya's new tutor, twenties

Shpigelsky
a doctor

Bolshintsov
a rich neighbour

Matvey
a servant

Katya
a maidservant

Arkady's country estate, Russia. Inside and out.

Three days in the mid-nineteenth century.

Summer.

.

THREE DAYS IN THE COUNTRY

One

Veranda of my country estate [handwritten]

~~The drawing room.~~ *Late afternoon.*

Schaaf, Anna and Lizaveta at a baize table playing cards.
    Natalya lies on a sofa, reading a novel. Rakitin
watches her. patio [handwritten]

Rakitin You haven't turned a page for ten minutes.

Natalya I'm a slow reader.

Rakitin No you're not.

> *Natalya turns a page, continues to read. Rakitin*
> *watches.*

Schaaf Hearts!

Anna Again?

Schaaf Yes. I have the hearts.

Anna You're a lucky old devil.

Lizaveta Our pain is his pleasure.

Schaaf Play, good ladies.

Anna Be warned, Professor, you'll scare us off.

> *Schaaf lays a card down, takes the trick.*

Lizaveta He's a demon!

Schaaf It is only money.

> *Lizaveta writes down the score in a small notebook.*
> *Schaaf shuffles the cards and they continue to play.*

Natalya Must you stand there?

3

Rakitin I'm your guest, you invited me here! You summoned me, three days ago.

Back at the card table:

Schaaf Hearts!

Anna Not again?

Lizaveta His luck is both disturbing and suspicious.

Anna (*to Natalya*) Natasha, sevens and eights are pouring out of him!

Lizaveta He bleeds hearts!

Natalya You lose every day – stop playing with him!

Schaaf No! They like to suffer, it is a peculiarity of the female.

Their game continues.

Natalya (*to Rakitin*) Did you see my husband?

Rakitin He's down at the weir. He was explaining a seemingly complicated detail to the workmen. To clarify his point he waded in, right up to his waist. *anglias*

Natalya Well, he does like to slosh about. *less interested in clothing. loves estate*

Rakitin The men were astonished.

Anna Where's Kolya?

Schaaf Where indeed? The boy is late for my tutorial.

Lizaveta Late? That's odd; he *lives* for his German lessons.

Natalya They went for a walk. He'll be back.

Schaaf (*to Lizaveta*) You to play, good lady.

The game continues.

Natalya Were you in Petersburg?

Rakitin Yes. Some business.

Natalya And some pleasure?

Rakitin No one you know. Then I journeyed to the Krinitsyns and endured a memorably unpleasant fortnight.

Natalya Tell me all.

Rakitin The Krinitsyns are young, beautiful, married a year . . . and they want to kill each other. By next spring their mutual loathing will have blossomed. By winter their marriage will have frozen. And then they'll have some children.

Natalya How did you pass the time?

Rakitin We drank. He drinks

Natalya You explored the limits of country life.

Rakitin And then I received your letter. Why did you send for me?

Natalya I don't remember.

Rakitin You wrote, 'I'm in despair, please come at once.'

Natalya You should've ignored me.

Rakitin You know I can't.

Natalya Ignore me!

At the card table:

Lizaveta Ha! He's lost a trick!

Anna He's defeated!

Lizaveta and Anna chuckle. Kolya comes in with a bow and arrow. He sees Natalya with Rakitin and heads towards Anna instead.

Kolya Grandma.

He presents the bow and arrow.

Anna What a fine weapon. Who made it?

Belyaev and Vera appear in the doorway. They stand there, golden.

Kolya (*points to Belyaev*) He did. He took his knife and some hazel and just did it. The arrow head is very sharp, it's flint.

Anna touches the point, pretends to be hurt.

Anna Oww! It's *lethal*. You be careful.

Natalya May I see?

Kolya hands her the bow and arrow. She inspects it. Kolya watches, hoping she'll approve.

(*To Belyaev.*) It's beautifully made.

Everyone watches as Natalya pulls back the bow and releases. It thrums. She fires at Rakitin; he mimes a soft blow to the heart.

Natalya And now, your German lesson.

Schaaf rises from the card table.

Kolya But we're going to feed the horses. *Please!*

Natalya Vera, return this boy in ten minutes. Go!

Kolya is out of the door. Vera and Belyaev follow him. Schaaf sits.

Rakitin (*to Lizaveta*) Who was that?

Lizaveta The new tutor. *Belyaev*. He appeared a few weeks ago to 'supplement' Professor Schaaf. He's one of his former students from the university – his *protégé*.

Schaaf No, he is not! Ladies, do we play?

They resume their game. Shpigelsky enters, carrying a leather bag.

Matvey Doctor Shpigelsky has arrived.

Shpigelsky They can see that! And you don't announce a doctor. (*To Matvey.*) As well you know. (*To Anna.*) Dear lady, please tell me you're annihilating the German, tell me you've inserted a stake through his heart. *anti- German ?*

Anna He is staggering . . .

Lizaveta He totters . . .

Schaaf But he is not yet fallen.

Shpigelsky (*to Lizaveta*) Madam, I have some new pills for you. Oh, I like your – what would you call it?

Lizaveta . . . Clothing?

Shpigelsky And the way it has relationship with your hair.

He bows to Lizaveta then goes over to Natalya.

Madam. Are you well?

Natalya I had a fever but it passed.

Shpigelsky You should've sent for me!

Natalya There was some medicine from last time.

Shpigelsky They don't last for ever. Even the finest potions can separate. You give them a shake but the magic has evaporated. (*To Rakitin.*) Why are you sniggering? (*To Natalya.*) Please . . .

She offers her arm and he takes her pulse.

Hmm. *Nerves.* You gush. You're a spring. You don't walk enough. You need to run about.

Natalya Where?

7

Shpigelsky Scamper in the fields. Fill your delicate lungs with air. *Perspire.*

Rakitin You men of science are mightily impressive.

Shpigelsky (*to Natalya*) May we speak in private?

Rakitin sighs, wanders off. Shpigelsky observes him a moment.

Each time I see him he's aged a decade.

Natalya To the matter.

Shpigelsky Your ward. The exquisite Vera. Subject: her future. A good and noble friend has asked me to discover your intentions.

Natalya He seeks her hand in marriage?

Shpigelsky You have it.

Natalya Who is he?

Shpigelsky My friend is one of your neighbours.

He vaguely gestures in a northerly direction.

Natalya Bolshintsov? Neighbours

Shpigelsky I couldn't say.

Natalya Then how may I consider the proposal?

Pause.

Shpigelsky It's Bolshintsov.

Natalya Then it's 'no'. I'm insulted you think him worthy of Vera.

Shpigelsky I concede he lacks *your* natural grace but he's respectable, willing and very rich. I sense you're unmoved.

Natalya I am stone.

Shpigelsky Well, she'll have to marry someone.

Natalya Yes, but not anyone! Your friend is deadly. Do thank him for his unwelcome interest.

Vera enters with Kolya. He approaches Rakitin, confidentially.

Kolya Are you busy?

Rakitin No.

Kolya Please could you find me some glue?

Rakitin Yes.

He doesn't move.

Kolya Now?

Natalya Kolya!

Schaaf has risen from the card table.

Anna Professor, would you care to settle up?

Schaaf bows and hands over a few coins to Anna and Lizaveta.

Schaaf Tomorrow it will return to its owner. *smile*

He approaches Kolya.

Erlauben Sie, Master Kolya.

Kolya *Guten Tag*, Herr Professor.

Schaaf *Kommen Sie, mein Herr.*

He tries to lead Kolya off, Kolya slightly resists.

Natalya (*to Kolya*) You've been playing all day, go and learn something!

Kolya What, Mother? What must I learn?

Natalya Now: German. Later: manners.

Kolya (*to Rakitin*) Don't forget the glue.

Schaaf leads Kolya off. Rakitin exits.

Vera (*to Shpigelsky*) Good day, good Doctor.

Natalya You're flushed.

Vera I'm exhausted!

Vera flops on to a sofa. Natalya and Shpigelsky observe her.

Natalya A *child*.

Shpigelsky There's really no need.

Natalya It was a sordid proposal.

Shpigelsky We all have cause for shame but in this respect I don't. I must go and see your coachman.

Natalya What's wrong with him?

Shpigelsky Boils.

He starts to exit. Rakitin is entering with a pot of glue.

She's more volatile than usual. I assume you know why?

Rakitin You're the doctor.

Shpigelsky Ah, but you're the expert.

Shpigelsky exits. Anna and Lizaveta at the card table. Vera on the sofa. Natalya collects her book, sits, tries to read. Rakitin stands in the middle of the room. He watches Vera. Then Anna and Lizaveta. Then Natalya. They are still, languorous.

Rakitin Portrait. A country scene: 'Four Ladies and Man with Pot of Glue.'

Lizaveta Perhaps a stroll before dinner?

Anna No, I need a rest.

Lizaveta I'm glad to see Kolya so changed. A month ago he was permanently enraged. Nothing could cheer him. Well, *I* couldn't. But I'm appalling with children, I don't have the patience.

Anna They need you to devote your time. It requires sacrifice. All other gestures of love are irrelevant.

Anna watches Natalya, who stares at her book.

My husband had no time. Men rush about mistaking activity for *purpose*. And then they die, mystified: 'I've done nothing, I wasted my life.' You've been wise to avoid them.

Lizaveta I think they avoided me.

Anna It's a blessing.

Vera (*to Natalya*) What are you reading?

Natalya At the ball last week there was no one to talk to. I drifted around looking pitiful. A kindly old Countess with one rheumy eye decided to adopt me. At considerable length she told me of the slow, slow death of her beloved husband. I felt I had died with him. Her consolation has been this novel: 'You haven't read it? Oh, but you must. It's delightful.' Now I can say that I have and it's not.

She snaps the book shut. Vera chuckles.

Where's the tutor?

Vera He went to wash himself.

Natalya Why?

Vera We were crossing the field, to the stables. He crept up on a cow and jumped on its back. It started running and bucking. Belyaev was thrown in the air. He fell in a most inconvenient place. Kolya said, 'At least it was a soft landing.'

She chortles. Natalya stands, paces a little.

Natalya The animal was frightened, he shouldn't have upset it.

Vera I know. But it was funny.

Natalya You might want to change for dinner.

Vera gets up. Natalya kisses her forehead.

Natalya You look very pretty today.

Vera goes to leave. Rakitin passes her the glue. They share a little joke and Vera exits.

Anna Natasha, what did the doctor want?

Natalya Nothing at all.

Anna He's a pest. (*Stares a moment.*) You're too pale.

Anna and Lizaveta exit.
  Natalya dismisses Matvey and Katya.
  Rakitin and Natalya are alone.

Natalya I'm too pale.

Rakitin Why did you send for me?

Natalya Too pale for what?

Rakitin Why?

She holds out her hand, he presses it. Tenderly.

Natalya You're too kind. Too constant. You shame me. Please don't look at me like that.

Rakitin I can't help my face. I'll do what I can with my countenance. But my feelings won't change.

Natalya You're condemned.

Rakitin I'm grateful to be certain of something in this world. You're an angel.

Natalya I'm really not.

Rakitin And yet you are.

I see myself on that street in Moscow. With your ~~Rat &~~ *I were* husband. Two young men. ~~Twenty~~ years ago. 'Look.' He *21.* nudged me. 'Look.' I looked: *you.* Walking your little dog. Your proud, tender praise as it cocked its leg. As if he'd performed a miracle. Arkady said, 'I don't care who she is or where she's from, I'm going to marry that woman.' You were fifteen seconds away from us. I failed to speak, to contest his position. Fifteen seconds. ~~Twenty~~ *12* years. And here we are.

Natalya You misremember. *Irritated, but running*

Rakitin No I don't. *he weir is still far for me*

Natalya There was no leg-cocking. She was a bitch.

Arkady enters, clothes still wet from the weir. He fixes himself a drink. *+ don't grab* *table glass, grab vodka*

Arkady I have great respect for the Russian peasant. He is resourceful and he is shrewd. But you explain a thing to him – he nods – you communicate in precise detail that which is required – he nods – you reiterate the supreme importance of the instruction and he nods *decisively* – he's got it. And then he simply doesn't do it. Hasn't started. It's as if the conversation never occurred. 'But it was yesterday, I told you specifically, you nodded.' 'Did *idiot* I?' '*Yes!*' 'Very sorry, will you explain it again, *Master?*' The sarcasm he engenders in that one word. They mock me every day – but with such invention I can't help admiring it. *Good at job?*

Rakitin Why don't you let the river flow as it demands?

Arkady Because it floods the damn field. Has done for centuries. I promised my father I'd deal with it.

Matvey enters, hands Arkady some linen to clean himself with.

13

It's not difficult to build a weir. Give me Germans, we'd do it in a week. The German *likes* to work; he listens, learns, wants to get it right. The Russian prides himself on getting it wrong.

Waves away Matvey, who exits.

Don't laugh, I'm in mortal pain!

Rakitin That's why I'm laughing.

Arkady It's all your fault.

Rakitin Oh, naturally.

Arkady The day I inherited this you should've counselled me to stay in the city.

Rakitin I did!

Arkady But you didn't assert it! You should've taken me by the throat and said, 'In the name of all that is holy don't go and live in the country.'

Rakitin You love it here.

Arkady Not today.

Belyaev enters.

You've been over to the barn?

Belyaev Yes, sir.

Arkady Are they still struggling with the first frame?

Belyaev No, sir, they've started on the third.

Arkady And the log-sets, did you tell them how I want it done?

Belyaev . . . Yes, sir.

Arkady (*sighs*) What did they say?

14

How long in charge?

Belyaev They said that four logs lashed horizontally is their practice and tradition. They suggested that no other method will work.

Arkady _My_ method.

New method.

Wants to make his mark w/ new.

Belyaev They communicated – firmly – that all other methods are destined for disaster.

Arkady (*to Rakitin*) Have I shown you my _new_ winnowing machine?

excited, new P55

Rakitin I think I'd remember if you had.

Arkady Well you must come now. It produces a hurricane – blow your head off.

Rakitin Oh, good.

    Rakitin and Arkady make to exit. Arkady turns back.

Arkady Do you want to come?

Natalya I've seen it.

Arkady Have you?

Natalya Yes.

    Arkady and Rakitin exit. Belyaev faces Natalya, about to exit.

Why did you jump on a cow?

Belyaev To amuse Kolya.

Natalya It's wrong. You do know that? It is simply wrong to jump on a cow.

Belyaev My apologies.

    Pause.

Natalya Your room and so on. All to your satisfaction?

Belyaev I've never lived anywhere so beautiful.

Natalya Yes, I thought that once. And my son?

15

Belyaev I like him very much.

Natalya Is he learning anything?

Belyaev hesitates.

You may speak freely.

Belyaev He's not confident. But he's responding well to encouragement. And he has a great spirit. I can see potential.

Natalya Before you came . . . he was a little withdrawn. My husband has the estate to oversee . . . and . . . we're neither of us as . . . present as we might be. As a child needs.

I've been unwell. I was.

I want Kolya to remember his childhood as . . .

I've been distracted. I fear it's affected him. How could it not?

We've neglected him. You've transformed him.

Please continue to be sensitive to his needs.

Belyaev I will.

Natalya Then again, those people who say they had a golden childhood. What on earth were they doing?

She stares at Belyaev, then looks away.

Whenever my father called us to his study . . . my brother and I would cross ourselves in terror. Once my brother grew up he broke with him. Never spoke to him again. But I stayed . . . and I longed for his return.

She is momentarily stricken, vulnerable. Belyaev makes a slight move towards her, she stops him with a gesture.

Natalya My father went blind. He became fond and kind. But I was still scared of him. When he held me, even as he murmured his love, I was taut with fear. I was never free in his presence.

16

He's dead.
   People fear me as I feared him.
   Are you afraid of me?

Belyaev I'm a little afraid. I hope appropriately so, given our positions.

Natalya Were you afraid of your father?

Belyaev I barely knew my parents.

Natalya Why?

Belyaev My mother died when I was five. And my father was always travelling. He still is. He makes a mess of things and scurries back.

Natalya Does he have a profession?

Belyaev To be polite, he's alert to opportunity. To be blunt, he's a thief.

Natalya He's a robber?

Belyaev A fraudster.

Natalya You've been unfortunate.

Belyaev I've always longed for someone to show me how to behave; rules of engagement, manners. I can barely handle the cutlery.

Natalya We will teach you.

Belyaev There are so many knives.

   Pause.

Natalya Was it you last night? By the lake.

Belyaev Ah. I'm afraid it was.

Natalya I was alone, outside. Your voice carried.

Belyaev My apologies for disturbing you.

Natalya You didn't. You sing well.

She holds out her hand. Belyaev takes it but isn't sure what to do with it. He bows to it and kisses it. Then straightens up.

When I offer my hand the convention is to press it.

Belyaev nods, embarrassed. Shpigelsky enters.

Shpigelsky I enter the servants' quarters in search of the agonised coachman; 'Show me the boils,' let me attend to the deadly pustules that brought me ten miles on a sweltering day, the boils that almost killed my horse and ruptured my spine. But my patient is sat at the table wolfing down his dinner. 'I'm here to lance your boils.' 'Oh, they've cleared up,' he says. How am I to survive if people simply 'get better'!?

Belyaev is edging out of the door when Vera hurries in.

Vera Aleksey Nikolayich! Aleksey!

Natalya Don't run! Don't shout!

She stops when she sees Natalya.

Vera They want him to come.

Natalya Who?

Vera At the winnowing machine, they want him to see it.

Natalya No, we're having dinner.

Shpigelsky helps himself to a drink. Vera and Belyaev are together, sharing a joke. Natalya sees this, watches them.

Vera It's because one of my legs is shorter than the other.

Belyaev Which one?

Vera I won't say. It's only half an inch and I disguise it – heroically.

Belyaev smiles.

Natalya Katya.

Katya enters.

Katya Madam?

Natalya is still watching Vera with Belyaev.

Madam?

Natalya (*to Vera and Belyaev*) You can go in.

Vera and Belyaev exit. Katya waits.

Doctor. We must make amends for your wasted journey, will you join us?

Shpigelsky (*surprised*) I'd be honoured.

Natalya (*to Katya*) Tell them to set another place.

Katya exits. Natalya and Shpigelsky are alone.

Natalya Your friend . . . Bolshintsov.

Shpigelsky The wealthiest landowner in the region. Excluding your husband.

Natalya His character?

Shpigelsky A saint. A modest man of the soil.

Natalya Why Vera?

Shpigelsky He yearns for the warmth of a young woman as his sun begins to set.

Natalya Did he say that?

Shpigelsky No, I did. He's far less poetic.

She gives him her arm. They exit.

snuffs tobacco +
to short

19

Two

The garden. The following day. Noon.
Two stone benches.

Arkady alone, staring out at the landscape. Kolya stands
with his bow and arrow, watching Arkady.
Katya hurries through with a basket of freshly picked
raspberries. She sees Arkady, slows, exits. Matvey follows
after, in pursuit. Exits.

~~Kolya~~ Father. Have you seen my tutor?

Arkady No.

Kolya is about to go.

Kolya . . .

He gestures for Kolya to stand by his side. They look
out. Arkady points.

From the forest . . . to the river . . . to the woodland and
the far village. See the tower?

Kolya nods.

Twenty square miles. A thousand souls. *Ours.*

He stares, overwhelmed by the burden.

~~Kolya~~ I think he might be at the lake.

Arkady looks at Kolya a moment. Lizaveta enters.

Lizaveta (*to Kolya*) Your piano lesson.

Arkady gestures Kolya over to her. Arkady goes to
exit, turns.

Arkady (*to Lizaveta*) Is he making any progress? *[handwritten: empathy]*

Lizaveta It's a fiendish instrument for small hands.

Arkady My piano teacher used to say that I made it sound like a coffin, full of dead keys. (*To Kolya.*) Good luck. *[handwritten: empathy for Kolya... "I hope he's doing okay..."]*

He exits.

Lizaveta (*to Kolya*) Come along. One day you'll think this was heaven.

Lizaveta and Kolya exit.
    Katya runs in with her basket, pursued by Matvey.

Matvey But why?!

Katya I don't know.

Matvey When *will* you know?!

Katya I don't know!

Matvey sinks to the ground.

Oh, get up.

Matvey Not till you tell me *why*.

Matvey There are *people*! Get up! It's pathetic.

Matvey It's passion! Ever heard of it? Ever felt it? Three months ago we got engaged, now you tell me you're not sure. What *happened*?

Katya Life!

Matvey Yesterday you loved me, today you don't know. You're very cruel. Is it your mother? I thought she approved? She *does* – she said I'm your salvation!

Katya SHE DOESN'T KNOW ME!

Schaaf enters carrying his fishing rod and a box of tackle. He surveys the abject scene before him.

Schaaf A lady with red berries, a gentleman with tears. It can only mean Love.

He helps himself to a handful of berries from Katya's basket.

I forget, dear Katerine, what are these?

Katya Raspberries.

Schaaf Ah. (*Teaching her.*) *Die Himbeere. Eine Himbeere.*

Katya *Himbeere.*

Matvey Will you please leave us!

Schaaf I assure you I did not mean to intrude. But your private display of emotion is quite public.

Matvey gets to his feet as Natalya and Rakitin enter. Matvey bows to them and exits.

Natalya Fishing.

Schaaf How did you know?

Natalya Is that a new rod?

Schaaf I am eager to employ it.

Natalya Where's Kolya?

Schaaf If you listen, it is evident . . .

Still life as they all listen to the distant sound of clunky piano playing. Ten seconds.

Natalya Well, he tries.

Schaaf Madam Lizaveta tortures the boy and in turn he tortures Chopin.

Natalya May we join you on your fishing expedition?

Rakitin (*sotto*) What?

Schaaf You are most welcome. (*To Rakitin.*) You may assist to put the maggot on the hook.

They exit. Katya is alone. Sound of the piano, Lizaveta plays a sweet little tune full of romantic yearning. Katya knows the song and sings along, in Russian. She sings well.

Belyaev enters holding a red kite. He watches Katya. After a while she sees him and stops singing.

Belyaev Don't stop.

Katya bows her head, embarrassed.

I like your voice.

Katya shrugs.

May I have one?

He points to the raspberries. Katya comes over to him, slowly.

Katya Have them all.

She puts the basket in his hands. They look at each other. A long look.
Vera enters holding the pot of glue and a hand-made tail for the kite.
Katya sees Vera, indicates with a nod that they're not alone.

Belyaev (*to Vera*) Would you like one?   raspberries = her love

Vera No, thank you.

She nods to Katya, who exits. Belyaev leaves the basket on a bench.

Belyaev What a fine tail.

Vera It's taken me two hours.

Belyaev Here.

She puts the pot of glue on the bench. Belyaev lays the kite on the bench and begins to attach the string to it.

Vera Do you ever fly a kite in Moscow?

Belyaev . . . No. No time.

Vera What keeps you so busy?

Belyaev Oh . . . reading. Thinking.

Vera Is that all?

Belyaev . . . Sometimes I write things.

Vera You write?

Belyaev Oh, nothing of value.

Vera You're a writer. You never said.

Belyaev It's just the occasional article or essay.

Vera For newspapers and periodicals?

Belyaev Yes.

Vera And they publish them?

Belyaev No.

He checks the kite, dabs glue here and there.

Vera Well, I'm sure they will.
I imagine you . . .

He looks at her, quizzically.

I imagine you work very hard. Late at night. With a stubby little candle on your desk.

Belyaev I have to work hard. Because I'm not very clever. Really! I spent most of my time at that desk with my forehead upon it.
I am ready for your tail.

She brings the tail and lays it to the kite. They begin to attach it.

Vera Do you have close friends in Moscow?

Belyaev . . . One or two.

Vera I have none at all. I don't know a soul.

Belyaev Well, *here*, who would you *want* to know? In the country – I didn't mean in this house.

Vera There's no one. (*Stares at him.*) Do you write poetry?

Belyaev Never.

Vera There was a girl at our school who wrote poems. She would read us her long, passionate poems in the dormitory at night. And we would weep.

Belyaev They were good?

Vera No. We cried out of pity. She couldn't write at all. We were sorry for her. And we guiltily howled into our pillows. She was so serious. And determined. She was convinced of her destiny. She wrote terrible poetry every day for two years. I'm boring you.

A distant strain of Kolya's piano playing.

Belyaev I hope it flies. We mustn't disappoint the young master.

Vera I love Kolya. I just love him.

Belyaev smiles, endeared. The kite is finished.

Belyaev May I ask how you know Natalya Petrovna?

Vera I've known her all my life. Her family adopted me. You see . . . Natalya Petrovna's father was fond of a particular servant in their household . . . and I . . . am the unwanted consequence of that fondness.

Belyaev Did you know your mother?

Vera (*shakes her head*) She died when I was born. But one mustn't spend one's life in mourning.

Belyaev And yet one does. Or can. I grieve for my mother but I barely remember her. And I grieve for my father and he's alive.

It's strange. I can't remember how long I've been here.

Vera Twenty-eight days.

She holds the kite aloft. Belyaev is holding the string. A long length, taut between them.

Shall we go and fly it?

Belyaev We must.

Vera Shall we go to the meadow?

They look at each other. A long look.

Belyaev We can fetch Kolya on the way.

Not fond of Vera.

Vera conceals her disappointment. As they exit with the kite, Natalya and Rakitin are entering.

Natalya Were they fleeing from us?

Rakitin Can you blame them?

Natalya She shouldn't be alone with him – oh, listen to me.

Rakitin Have you warned the tutor off?

Natalya He's not a savage, he'll know she's forbidden. But I'll have to talk to her.

Rakitin (*sotto*) Poor Vera.

Natalya Why 'poor Vera'?

Rakitin I take it back.

Natalya I'm not a dragon.

Rakitin I meant no offence.

Natalya Offence has been taken. You're in my garden enjoying my hospitality. Don't mock me!

She pokes him angrily with the tip of her parasol. He looks chastened.

(*Laughing.*) I didn't mean it! (*As if to a baby.*) Ooh. Ooooh. Come here. Oh, come here. *Come!*

Rakitin does so.

Your cheek. Offer it. Please.

He offers it. She kisses it.

Better?

Rakitin Do it again.

She kisses his cheek.

Better.

Natalya What's wrong with me?

Rakitin I really don't know. But I preferred it a month ago when you were simply sad.

Natalya Those were the days.

Rakitin (*gazes at her*) What troubles you so? Tell me.

Natalya It'll pass.

Pause.

Rakitin Why don't we go somewhere?

Natalya It's too hot.

Rakitin Let's visit someone, let's *descend.*

Natalya What do you think of Bolshintsov?

Rakitin (*thinks a moment*) He's a dullard. Meeting him is the same as not meeting him.

Natalya When *did* you meet him?

Rakitin The winter before last, he played Preference with the ladies. They destroyed him.

Natalya Perhaps he let them, perhaps he has good manners?

Rakitin Why does it matter?

Natalya It doesn't!

Rakitin I don't know what he's like. I haven't studied the gentleman. But should you wish me to conduct a clandestine observation I am, as ever, at your service.

He glances at Natalya. She's looking into the distance.

Are you looking at the oak tree?

She nods, overcome with sadness. Unseen by him.

I've always loved that oak. The darkest green against the bluest sky. Perfect shape. Perfect solitude. You couldn't paint it. You'd only fail it. The lone oak, the long line of birch behind it. A hundred silver stakes in the earth. The tiny leaves sparkling and melting in light. Such majesty.

Natalya You're so refined. You pay court to Nature like a perfumed marquis deigning to seduce a peasant. Birch trees don't melt and swoon like febrile young women. The oak is not alone 'philosophically'. It's alone because a rough farmer made it so two centuries ago. It's alone because it's alone!

Rakitin *Quelle tirade.*

They stare out at the landscape.

Natalya We're as old as those hills, old friend.

Rakitin I'm not. Nor are you.

Natalya . . . But it seems so long since we were young . . .

Rakitin ... This will be my last summer. *Ultimatum*.

Pause.

Natalya They sat here. It's a furnace. You could fry an egg on it.

Rakitin When did you ever fry an egg?

Natalya In my youth.

Rakitin I don't envy them. Nor the shock of pain awaiting them. Who'd want that again?

Natalya Anyone who wanted to *live*! From now on I suggest we abandon our discourses on nature and love. I must go and talk to Vera.

Not unrequited. Not to Rak.

Rakitin looks upset.

Don't make this mean something.

She exits. Rakitin looks around, then takes out his handkerchief, wipes his eyes. Belyaev enters.

Belyaev Excuse me, sir. Do you know where I can buy some gunpowder?

Rakitin stares at Belyaev, suddenly considering him.

Rakitin At the shop in town. They sell it under the counter. Tell them you'd like some 'poppyseed'. It's code. You can wink if you want.

Belyaev Thank you, sir.

Rakitin Are you going to blow us all to bits?

Belyaev (*laughs*) I'm going to make some fireworks. For Natalya Petrovna's name day. I'm planning a display by the lake. I've thought of a way to float Roman candles. Fire on water. Do you think she'd like that?

christening / name day

Rakitin I think she'd go wild.

29

Pause.

Belyaev I saw you were engrossed in *The Contemporary* last night . . . I used to read it in Moscow – whenever I could get a copy . . .

Rakitin Would you like to borrow it?

Belyaev Could I?

Rakitin Do you favour its art or its politics?

Belyaev The latter. I'd like to read their tribute to Belinsky.

Rakitin Ah. Of course.

Belyaev You're not an admirer?

Rakitin I respected the man but his politics bore me. I'm frivolous. You disapprove.

Belyaev (*smiles*) I do, sir.

Rakitin Socialism. Freedom for the serfs. Once they're freed, will they really be free? None of us are free.

Belyaev Hence the longing, sir.

Rakitin smiles, conceding the point.

When I was a student Belinsky gave a lecture. There were hundreds of us, crammed into the hall. And he held us . . . *raised* us. He was free. He had such *fire* . . . I've known that urge . . . to burn it down.

Rakitin What, exactly?

Belyaev The urge is quite vague.

Rakitin Do warn us if it assumes a focus.

They look at each other.

I'm told you tinker? (*Gestures, 'writing'.*)

Belyaev No. I have no talent for anything meaningful.

Rakitin Teaching requires talent. I hear you're very good at it. You strike me as highly competent in a number of fields.

Belyaev Ha! I'm really not!

Rakitin I can't decide! Are you a blunderer or an assassin? Competition

Pause. for Nat.

Belyaev Have I missed something?

Rakitin I don't know, have you?

Pause.

Belyaev Did you hear that?

They listen. They hear the distinctive call.

It's a corncrake. I'll get my gun.

Natalya is entering.

Rakitin I wouldn't. She can't abide blood sports. Or so she claims.

Natalya We're waiting for you!

Rakitin stares at her. She smiles at him. Vera and Kolya are behind her in the distance.

We're going to the meadow. To fly the kite!

She offers her hand. Rakitin instinctively advances and then regrets it. She meant it for Belyaev who now takes her arm.

(*To Belyaev.*) If I offer my hand, you should take it like this. If I offer my arm, you must take it like this.

They exit, talking. Rakitin watches them.

Rakitin goes over to a bench and sits with the basket of raspberries. He's in despair. He picks out a big raspberry and contemplates it.

Rakitin Be poisoned. Take me. Do it now.

Katya runs past and straight off, in a state of agitation. Then Matvey follows, equally agitated. He stops. Gets his breath.

Matvey A stitch! (*Bows.*) Sir. She just blurted it out, freely confessed it! She's in love with the tutor!

Rakitin Well, Professor Schaaf is a very dark horse.

Matvey No! The *other* tutor! (*Flatly.*) Oh. Very good. Why don't people take me seriously?

Rakitin Everyone's a joke they don't get.

Matvey Should I chase after her?

Rakitin To what end? 'Here is my heart, will you stamp on it some more, please?' Leave her alone, take a cold bath and pray he has no feelings for her.

Matvey You're right. Thank you, sir. Good advice.

He thinks, then dashes after Katya.

Katya! Katya!

Rakitin eats another raspberry. Then another. They're delicious.

Rakitin (*softly*) Good old life.

He spots two men. He groans. Shpigelsky and Bolshintsov enter.

Shpigelsky Rakitin! Are you brooding? Yes, he's in one of his sombre moods. Shall we pass through?

Rakitin Do as you please.

Shpigelsky Natalya Petrovna has kindly invited us to lunch.

Rakitin They're up in the meadow. Didn't you see them from the house?

Shpigelsky No . . . we came via the copse. *(trees)*

Rakitin Why?

Shpigelsky Bolshintsov wanted to see if there were any mushrooms there. He adores them.

Bolshintsov looks embarrassed.

Rakitin I trust you wouldn't pick a mushroom without Arkady's permission? *I might be picky about tampering w/ nature.*

Shpigelsky Ah, in this region, the fungi within a neighbour's copse are considered fair game. I thought you'd know.

Rakitin No, I'm not familiar with the custom of the mushroom.

Shpigelsky Well, we have observed it.

Rakitin And feasted accordingly.

Shpigelsky No! There were none that attracted him, he's most particular.

Rakitin observes Bolshintsov eyeing the basket.

Rakitin Are you peckish?

He offers up the basket.

Bolshintsov Thank you. You're most generous.

He helps himself to a handful. So does Shpigelsky. Rakitin likewise. The three men eat raspberries in silence. After a while:.

Shpigelsky These are astonishing.

Bolshintsov has a full mouth. He nods, approvingly.

Rakitin I might take some down to Arkady, at the weir.

Rakitin tries to take the basket from Shpigelsky – he's reluctant.

Give.

Shpigelsky releases.

See you at lunch.

Rakitin exits with the basket.

Bolshintsov Why did you say that? Now he thinks I'm a mushroom stealer!

Shpigelsky What *he* thinks is of no importance!

Bolshintsov But it's not true, I hate mushrooms!

Shpigelsky It just came to me! Would you prefer it if I'd told him the truth? 'No, we didn't notice them up in the meadow because Bolshintsov had an attack of nervous palpitations at the gate and needed to recover in the garden'? Better a mushroom thief than a gibbering social cripple – not that you are one. Now let's get this thing whirring!

Bolshintsov I wish he hadn't taken those raspberries, suppose my empty belly embarrasses me at the table?

Shpigelsky Please stop *worrying*! It's going *well*! Last night, after dinner, Natalya Petrovna's exact words: 'Bring him to lunch. Should he earn Vera's affection I will not oppose their happiness.'

Bolshintsov 'Will not oppose their happiness.' Why not?

Shpigelsky Why would she? It's a perfect union of youth and beauty conjoined with . . . wisdom and experience.

Bolshintsov And you're certain that Natalya Petrovna approves of me?

Shpigelsky She is prepared to.

Bolshintsov I wish I approved of myself!

Shpigelsky You charged me to plead your case – this I have done with *zeal* – now let's see some action from *you*! The girl is not a goddess, she's lonely and soulful – always was – she's ripe for the picking. Now we must make our way *indoors*.

Bolshintsov Right.

Shpigelsky starts to usher Bolshintsov towards the house.

Shpigelsky Oh, one last thing: don't worry about the physical aspect.

Bolshintsov I'm sorry?

Shpigelsky How you look, don't fret about it.

Bolshintsov Wha—?

Shpigelsky They don't care – not as much as one thinks.

Bolshintsov has stopped.

Bolshintsov My friend. As you rightly say, I did ask you to engineer an opportunity –

Shpigelsky 'Ask'? You demanded, you *importuned* – and we cut a *deal*.

Bolshintsov I know! But I can't do this, I want to go home!

Shpigelsky Fine. Tomorrow I will be compelled to tell Natalya Petrovna that you refused her generous invitation to lunch due to an overwhelming bout of cowardice.

Bolshintsov Couldn't you say I was ill?

Shpigelsky But you're not! I'm not a *liar*, I don't lie to my esteemed patients! Not as a habit.

Bolshintsov I'm going home.

Shpigelsky stops him and stares.

Shpigelsky Untended grave. Moss. Droppings. Here lies Bolshintsov: 'He lived alone, produced no heir and his wealth died with him.'
'How is this so?'
'Oh, he wouldn't have lunch.'
Come on, let's cluck our way out of here.

Bolshintsov Wait! Let me explain. My friend – may I say my *best* friend.

Shpigelsky (*astonished*) Really?

Bolshintsov I have to tell you something, my deepest secret.

Shpigelsky (*tersely*) Oh, can't it wait? Tell me in the carriage.

Bolshintsov NO, IT CAN'T WAIT!

Shpigelsky jumps in alarm.

My adult life has been devoted to my estate . . . I've had almost no 'contact' with the ladies – or with the feminine race in general. I've not . . . *mingled*.

Shpigelsky Are you saying you're a virgin?

Bolshintsov No! There are women in the town who I have . . . 'visited'. But I'm inept in the art of *romance*. I can't think of a thing to say to Miss Vera!

Shpigelsky Then let *her* talk! They love to witter on. You must simply be a good ear – strong – silent. And nod now and then to prove you're listening.

Bolshintsov But can't you furnish me with an amusing remark – to get me *started*?

Shpigelsky You can't rehearse wit, she'll hear the cogs grinding! Oh, you're so humble! You inherited a failing estate and turned it round – be *proud* – you're a *leader*. Why in your mighty soul do you fear these minor gentry? You're a better man than any of 'em. Moreover, you have three hundred serfs. *I have more.*

Bolshintsov Three hundred and twenty.

Shpigelsky There! So why be afraid?

Bolshintsov Because I'm shy. Because I'm too old for her. Because this whole escapade is folly. Because I don't know 'women'!

Shpigelsky Embrace it as an asset! You're *innocent* – free of cynicism – you've not been kicked to death by love's black boot – what other man on this *planet* can offer that?!

Bolshintsov It's a point.

Shpigelsky It's a huge point. Now – *concentrate*: after lunch you will lure her to a private place and you will say: 'Vera. My admiration for you is . . . colossal. I am asking for the honour of your hand. Were you to marry me you would be rich and revered. Give me your answer when you please. I am prepared to wait. And I shall consider it a privilege so to do.'

Shpigelsky basks a moment.

Bolshintsov Mmm. That's *good*. One thing: the 'waiting'.

Shpigelsky What of it?

Bolshintsov I can't wait for ever, shouldn't there be a limit?

Shpigelsky How long would you suggest?

Bolshintsov Erm . . . a week?

Shpigelsky hoots.

A month?

More hoots.

Surely not a *year*? Help me or to hell with our deal!

Shpigelsky You will wait *indefinitely* for your future wife.

Natalya, Belyaev, Vera and Kolya come running in, with the kite, all laughing and shouting. They run past Shpigelsky and Bolshintsov.
Bolshintsov gazes at Vera. Kolya launches the kite. It flies.

Bolshintsov I'm in love.

transition: Open doors w/ flowerpot + lanterns

Three

Veranda

~~The drawing room.~~ *That night.*

Schaaf asleep on the sofa. A near empty glass of wine in his hand. Bolshintsov is sitting at the card table, nursing a drink. Shpigelsky, quite drunk, stands in profile, downing a glass of red. Matvey waits with the bottle. The only movement is the slow pulse of the wine as Shpigelsky drains the glass.

Shpigelsky Give me the bottle.

Matvey holds on to it. Shpigelsky eyes him.

Matvey Doctor. Do you have anything I can take for severe emotional pain?

Shpigelsky Yes, an overdose of sleeping pills. Now give me the bottle.

Matvey hands it over and exits.

Bolshintsov This day has been a disaster. I'm hopeless. There's no hope.

Shpigelsky My dear friend, there is always hope.

Bolshintsov People only say that when they know it's not true.
I wish I could kill myself.
But I have too many responsibilities.
I will leave at dawn.

Rakitin comes in. Bolshintsov rises, bows to both and exits.

Rakitin Well?

39

Shpigelsky A favour.

Shpigelsky points to where Bolshintsov exited.

Rakitin He's a fool – and so are you for getting involved.

Shpigelsky My kind heart will be my ruination. Yes, he's a fool, but since when was marriage the province of the wise? You can't prevent fools from marrying, nor from procreating – nor should you! The world needs its idiots more than its intelligentsia.

He hands Rakitin a glass of wine.

After lunch this afternoon: 'How dare you bring that hog to my house and dangle him at Vera.' 'But dear Natalya Petrovna, dear, dear lady, you *invited* us! You – you – you!' An hour later she commands us to stay for *dinner*, says we 'simply *must*'. Then, she places Bolshintsov down at the boring end with the tutors and the boy while Vera's up at the top beseated on a distant continent. After dinner she says, 'Oh but you have to stay the night, we've hardly *seen* you!' She's insane!

Rakitin (*warning*) Be careful.

Shpigelsky How I pity the husband. No wonder he's barely here. A busy worker bee avoiding the queen.

Rakitin Why are you helping Bolshintsov? It's out of character.

Shpigelsky Everyone's out of character. Always.

Rakitin What's he paying you?

Shpigelsky (*innocently*) Hmm?

Rakitin stares at him.

Nothing. He's a dear friend!

Rakitin stares.

My faithful horse is going lame. A country doctor with a bad horse might as well be dead.

Rakitin And he's promised you a new one.

Shpigelsky Three actually.

Rakitin laughs. Shpigelsky takes Schaaf's wine glass and downs the dregs. He puts the glass back in Schaaf's hand, then quickly checks Schaaf's pulse.

Three black mares. The most beautiful creatures I've ever seen. Even *you* would kneel before them. (*Offers snuff.*) A pinch?

Rakitin I've been refusing your snuff for close to a decade, why do you persist?

Shpigelsky It's what we do, it's our routine.

Rakitin And if I said yes?

Shpigelsky I'd be offended.

He snorts a load. Rakitin watches, concealing his revulsion.

Rakitin Well?

Shpigelsky Natalya Petrovna respects you, get her to behave rationally, give the poor man a *chance*. Whenever she explodes Bolshintsov pleads to go home and another horse bolts.

Rakitin In what possible universe would Vera marry him?

Shpigelsky In a wretched one – *this* one! (*Looks off.*) She's coming! I'm going to bed.

Hurries to exit, then turns.

Why are the sheets so cold here?

Shpigelsky exits as Natalya enters from elsewhere.

Natalya I have to talk to you.

Rakitin points to the sleeping Schaaf. Natalya prods the tutor, who wakes with a startled exclamation.

Natalya Professor! Bedtime.

Schaaf stumbles out, still half asleep, muttering in German.

I've mistreated you. Today, yesterday. Before.
Whatever I say or might do . . . there is no one I love as I love you.

She takes Rakitin's hand, kisses it once. He gazes at her. Resists the instinct to speak.

I know you value my honesty. But it will hurt you. Yet I think you're more hurt by what I conceal from you than what I confess: I like Belyaev. I think of him. Often. Too much.

Pause.

Rakitin I know.
And, now, you will tell me it's a ridiculous infatuation.

Natalya . . . Yes.

She bows her head in shame.

Rakitin He's half your age.

Natalya Not quite.

Rakitin He's a member of your staff. He tutors your son. It's unthinkable.

Natalya (*forcefully*) I think of him.

Rakitin turns away in pain.

I can't compose myself. Dear friend, I need your help.

Rakitin I can't. You're alone.

Natalya Nothing has happened.

Rakitin Oh, does it matter?

Natalya *He* doesn't know. No one *knows*. Help me be rid of it. Counsel me!

Rakitin Resist it.

Natalya I can't.

Rakitin Resist it!

Natalya I've tried. But I have such thoughts – dreams – violent need.

Rakitin Enough! I cannot be of assistance in this matter. You know why.
  The doctor is perplexed by your storms. He's asked me to navigate. May Bolshintsov continue to court Vera? Your answer, please.

Natalya I can't bear your anger.

Rakitin Your answer.

Natalya I can't answer. I need to speak to Vera.

Rakitin Then I'll bring her to you.

Natalya Now?

Rakitin Why not? (*Goes to exit.*) You bid me send her to you?

Natalya Please don't abandon me.

Rakitin Do you bid me?

Natalya I shouldn't have spoken.

Rakitin (*coldly*) Do you bid me?

Natalya Yes.

Rakitin exits. Natalya stands, motionless.
Vera enters, nervously.

It's my duty to inform you of a proposal. I've been asked for your hand in marriage.

Vera is stunned – and now hopeful . . .

It's not surprising; you're unspoiled and young and we live in a wilderness. Do you think you're ready to marry?

Vera Yes.

Natalya I'm not sure this man is worthy of you. But I believe he's decent and honest and if you like him I would give my consent.

Vera I do like him.

Pause.

Natalya I haven't told you who he is.

Vera I know who he is.

Natalya How?

Vera What did he say?

Natalya . . . He said that from the moment he met you, he's been smitten. He returned today and declared his love.

Vera (*confused*) Who did?

Natalya Your suitor.

Vera He 'returned'?

Natalya The doctor's friend.

Vera Who?

Natalya Bolshintsov! He wants to marry you!

Vera puts her hand to her mouth. Swallows. Swallows again.

I think your feelings are clear. *Now.*

Vera Please don't make me marry him!

Natalya Why would I?

Vera Because I'm a burden on the household. And I haven't been the companion you wanted.

Natalya There is no one who is that.

Vera Please don't make me!

Natalya Vera! I'm not your enemy!

Vera I know! I love you, I look up to you.

Natalya Well, you shouldn't. Not too much.

Vera Please don't make me.

Natalya Of course I won't!

Vera Thank you! Oh, thank you!

Natalya There.

Vera The thought of him touching me . . .

Natalya Bolshintsov can hawk his flesh elsewhere. We won't let him near this . . . overwhelming face.

She walks about, can't settle. Needs to know . . .

Is there a reason why he so disgusts you? A reason beyond his age and manner?

Vera Isn't that enough?

Natalya Yes, but he's not an ogre, your distaste is profound.

Vera I want to marry for love. As you did.

Pause.

Natalya Have you found a suitable candidate?

Vera . . . No.

Natalya At the Krinitsyns' wedding, you danced with that tall officer.

Vera No, I don't like him. There was a moment when I thought I did but then I didn't.

Natalya What about Shalansky?

Vera I think he likes Liza Velskaya.

Natalya Yes, I thought that too. How about Rakitin?

Vera No! I adore him, but he's like an uncle.

Natalya He's lonely.

Vera I think he likes to be.

Natalya You said 'I know who he is'. Who is he?

Vera No one.

Natalya The tutor?

Vera No.

Natalya He seems a fine young man. A touch reticent perhaps but quite charming.

Vera He's not reticent.

Natalya Shy then.

Vera That's because he's afraid of you.

Natalya How do you know?

Vera He told me.

Natalya You talk quite intimately?

Vera Oh, yes. I know he leaps about but in his heart he's gentle.

Natalya That huge ditch he bounded across . . .

Vera He's a panther!

Natalya Yes!

Vera He cheers me.

Natalya He fears me . . .

Vera I will tell him not to. I will tell him how kind you are.

   Natalya looks at Vera. A long look.

Natalya You can tell me . . .

Vera I'm in love with him. I love him passionately. I dream of him. Can I tell you? I know lust. And wildness. *Here.* (*Presses her stomach.*) I know it now, I know what poetry means.

Natalya Poetry.
   And he?
   Vera.
   And he?
   Verochka.
   And *he*?

Vera Yes. I think it's so. I believe he loves me. I believe so.

   Natalya is pale. Motionless.

You're white. Should I send for someone?

Natalya No.

Vera Have I upset you?

Natalya No.

Vera What should I do?

Natalya Leave me. Go, please.

   Vera exits. Natalya remains motionless. Rakitin
   hurries in.

Rakitin Vera says you're unwell. Natasha. I know that look.

She remains staring out.

Forgive me. I was cruel before.

And now you in turn, turn from me.

Ignore what I said. Let me continue to be your trusted friend.

I placed my pain above your need. I won't again. Forgive me.

Pause.

Natalya I'm sorry, I didn't hear a word of that.

Rakitin I made an apology.

Natalya Well, I'm sure it was gracious. What's wrong with me?

Rakitin You're in love. For the first time.

Natalya It's so late. And ludicrous.

Rakitin I know what should happen.

Natalya They're in love. She loves him. He loves her. It's *right*.

Rakitin Do you want my advice? Or do you want to stand there and flay yourself?

Natalya looks at him, smiles sadly.

Natalya Advice.

Rakitin On condition that you receive it in the spirit in which it is offered.

Natalya nods.

I want to help you and I want you to accept that.

Natalya nods.

I have no other purpose – even if it may seem otherwise.

Natalya Speak!

Rakitin Belyaev must leave. He must go in the morning. I'm not going to talk to you of your husband or your duty. From me such things are inappropriate and hypocritical. But Belyaev must leave.

Agreed?

Pause.

Natalya Yes.

Rakitin And I'll go with him. You won't see me again.

Natalya I would've married her off, I would've done anything to make him mine.

Rakitin I said, 'You won't see me again.' Ever.

Natalya doesn't respond.

Fine. So, the tutor, the suitor and the supplicant will be gone tomorrow. All gone.

Pause.

Natalya What will there be to live for?

Rakitin You'll get better.

Natalya Have *you*?

Rakitin I might now.

Natalya There's nothing here.

Pause.

Rakitin There's your husband.

Natalya (*softly*) Nothing.

Rakitin There's your son . . .

She looks down, ashamed.

Natalya This marriage. A performance of love. For a willing audience . . . of one small boy. *Reasons for staying together*

49

Rakitin If you wish it . . . I could stay on, for a day or two. To help you once he's gone . . .

Natalya Ah.

Rakitin If you wish it.

Natalya You have even less cunning than the doctor.

Rakitin I'm not plotting!

Natalya In mourning, she turns to her humble adviser. She succumbs to his deep understanding. Look how smoothly he wields a linen handkerchief.

Rakitin No!

Natalya You deceive yourself!

Rakitin I told you! I gave you my counsel with no other purpose! I'm trying to help you. Because I love you. Because I *truly* love you!

   But I see it now: you can't be loved. Not by me or anyone! You hate yourself. And anyone who dares to love you threatens the purity of your self-loathing.

She moves towards him. He holds his ground. She might hit him. But instead, she kisses him, passionately.

Anna comes in. Stops.

Anna (*whispers*) Natasha!

Arkady enters. Natalya and Rakitin part.

Arkady Just – don't – lie.   *fuming w/ anger*

Rakitin I'm leaving tomorrow. And I will explain. But I can't now.

Arkady I think you should – *now.*   Bullshit answers,

Rakitin It won't make sense.   more to Rakitin,

Arkady Natasha.   then Natalya

anchor when speaking

Natalya I was saying goodbye.

Arkady I asked you not to lie!

Natalya I was saying goodbye!

Arkady (to Anna and Rakitin) Please leave us.

Natalya No! We're still talking. It's *important*!

Anna (to Arkady) Let them!

Arkady Don't interfere!

Anna There's nothing to be done! Leave them alone!

> Anna exits. Arkady looks at Rakitin, then Natalya.
> They're unreachable. Arkady exits.
>   Rakitin stares at Natalya. Then raises an eyebrow.

Natalya Don't.

> He gestures, innocently.

Don't!

Rakitin Do you take me for a savage?

Natalya Don't!

Rakitin Do you think me so low that I would prospect for mirth in this barren place? Natalya Petrovna, there is no Mirth here. (*Mock grandiose.*) There is only Despair and Desolation.

> He giggles with glee. She tries to suppress her
> amusement but fails.
>   They laugh together, and then he gazes at her.

It was a nice kiss.

Natalya Oh. Good.

Rakitin It was the nicest kiss I've had for seven years. Was it nothing?

Natalya A kiss is never nothing.

Rakitin moves towards her.

But the fact remains.

Rakitin stops. They look at each other.

Rakitin It's a shame.

Natalya But there it is.

Pause.

Rakitin I'll talk to Belyaev. He'll understand. I'll tell him of Vera's feelings and that it's impossible for them to conduct a love affair while she is your ward and he is your employee. Can't be done. Best if he goes. Very sorry. Here's three month's wages. Farewell.

Natalya I'll tell him.

Rakitin You?

Natalya Will you find him, please?

Rakitin Now?

Natalya Yes, why not?

Rakitin You'll tell him to go.

Natalya Don't you trust me?

Pause.

Rakitin And we'll leave tomorrow. Me and him.

Natalya You can share a carriage.

Rakitin That'll be jolly.

Natalya Go and get him.

Rakitin makes to exit.

I'll miss you.

Rakitin exits. Natalya waits.

And if he loves her. As she loves him.
 What will I do?
 Kill myself.

Lizaveta enters.

Lizaveta Oh. I thought everyone had gone to bed.

Lizaveta searches for something.

Natalya Under the table.

Lizaveta Hmm?

Natalya Your snuff box.

Lizaveta Ah. My guilty secret.

Natalya It's hardly a secret.

Lizaveta It's a vile habit but it helps me through.
Goodnight.

Lizaveta exits. Natalya waits.

Natalya But I won't. I'll want to but I won't.
 No one dies of love.
 Do they?

Belyaev enters. Natalya stares at him.

Vera . . . is in love with you. Did you know?

Belyaev No.

Natalya Did you encourage her?

Belyaev No. She loves me?

Natalya Is it so strange?

Belyaev Is she upset?

Natalya Well, of course she is! Upset, elated, broken,
enraptured.

Belyaev She told you this?

Natalya She thinks of you in her sleep, her dreams, her waking moments. She is giddy. Like a girl. Like the girl she is.

She must understand I have a duty of care. What are your feelings for Vera? She has gained the impression that you're not indifferent to her.

Belyaev I'm not.

Natalya Not what?

Belyaev I'm not indifferent.

Natalya Do you love her? It's a simple question. Please provide the answer.

Do you love her?

Pause.

Belyaev No.

Natalya How do you know?

Belyaev How does anyone know?

Natalya Don't be obtuse!

Belyaev I don't love Vera in the way you have said she loves me.

Natalya You don't?

Belyaev No.

Natalya Might you, one day?

Belyaev No.

Natalya She said something about poetry.

Belyaev . . . There was a girl at her school who wrote poems. It was just a story she told.

Natalya Have you read to her? Written poems for her? Recited? Regaled? Have you encouraged her to perceive you as a romantic or poetic entity?

Belyaev No!

Natalya Well, these things happen. Don't blame yourself.

Belyaev Should I talk to her?

Natalya No! I will.

Belyaev I feel I should leave. I should go tomorrow.

Natalya I'll decide on that! You have a contract. Kolya needs you. You're necessary.

Belyaev I would be very sad to leave.

Natalya Why?

Belyaev I love this house. I've never been happier.

Natalya Why?

Belyaev I felt I belonged. But I've ruined it.

Natalya It doesn't follow that you should leave. I don't know what's best. I'll give you my decision in the morning.

Kolya comes in wearing his nightshirt.
He is muttering to himself in Russian. Gibberish.

Natalya (*whispering*) He sleepwalks. Did you know?

Belyaev shakes his head. They watch Kolya. The boy walks about the room. Then he sees Belyaev and runs into his arms.

Kolya My liege! My good and noble liege!

Belyaev holds Kolya, fondly.

Belyaev My Prince, 'tis most late this hour.

Natalya watches, moved.

Your mother is here.

Natalya comes over.

Kolya Do you love me?

Natalya Yes, my darling. Go back to bed.

Kolya Will you come and see me?

Natalya In a minute.

Kolya Both of you?

Kolya joins their hands.

Belyaev (*to Kolya*) Goodnight.

Natalya kisses Kolya and sends him off.
    They watch him go then turn to each other.

Natalya Vera says you're afraid of me.
I'm telling you this because . . .
I'm telling you this . . .
I'm telling you . . .
I tell you . . .
Look how dark it is.

Natalya gazes at him, entranced.

Belyaev She's wrong. I'm not afraid.

A moment. And then Belyaev exits.

Natalya goes to the candle on the card table.
    She puts her hand over the flame.
    She stands there for as long as she can bear.
    Then she lowers her hand and snuffs out the light.

Four

An abandoned glasshouse. Noon. The next day.

Stone floor. Old storage crates. Broken garden furniture. Upstage centre, an old, rough, heavy iron door leads to an unseen storeroom.

It's raining. Kolya stares at the iron door. He walks towards it, puts his ear to the door, listening. An exclamation from outside sends him running away.
   Shpigelsky and Lizaveta hurry in from the garden, taking shelter. They shake their clothes, hats, stamp a little.

Shpigelsky Summer!

   Shpigelsky flourishes a handkerchief, lays it down on a dusty crate.

Will you?

Lizaveta I appreciate the gesture but I don't want to spoil it.

Shpigelsky Your graciousness is noted. But do sit if you please.

   He paces a little, anxiously.

This shower has rather ruined the moment.

Lizaveta Was there one . . .?

   To her amazement he begins to lower himself on to one knee.

Shpigelsky Lizavetaaaaggghhh!!! Back – lower back. Seized! Iron fist squeezing the spine!

Lizaveta What can I do?

Shpigelsky Avoid laughter.

He struggles on the floor, gasps in pain.

Aaaggghh. Aaaaggghhh.

Lizaveta Do you need to sit?

Shpigelsky (*out of breath*) Can't sit. Hell to sit.
Do you suffer, with the back?

Lizaveta No, I'm quite supple. I did ballet as a girl.

Shpigelsky I imagine you were exquisite.

Lizaveta Not at all. I was a lumpy child. And my tread
was heavy. But I loved it. Until the dance master had a
quiet word with my mother.

Shpigelsky What a rotten man! I hate him! How bravely
you've transcended the pain he inflicted.

Lizaveta It was forty years ago.

Shpigelsky You're quite right, I was flattering you. Crate!

Lizaveta brings a crate to him. He eyes it.

Smaller.

*She brings him a smaller crate. He uses it to help him
stand.*

Ahhh. Uuueerrgghh. Oooooohhrr.

He catches his breath, still in pain, but it's receding.

Now . . . please imagine that I stand before you on one
knee. As it were. And I am saying, 'Lizaveta Bogdanovna,
will you do me the great honour of being my wife?' Please
don't answer! Not yet. There are things I am compelled
to *warn* you of, things pertaining to my circumstances
and my character.

Lizaveta May I take notes?

Shpigelsky Erm . . . fine. Provided I may refer to mine?

Lizaveta nods and takes out her notebook. Shpigelsky produces a sheaf of scribbled notes from his pocket.

My circumstances: I regret to inform you that I am of low birth. I'm not a peasant, I'm a notch above – but the notch is . . . negligible. I understand that you are not of great stock either?

Lizaveta That is correct.

Shpigelsky Yes, men like me must learn to lower our – our – you take my meaning?

Lizaveta It's perfectly clear.

She makes a firm note in her book.

Shpigelsky I – I simply meant that you've been 'family retainer' here for many years, it's therefore unsurprising that you exhibit some of the symptoms of spinsterhood – what I *mean* is that I detect there is still *life* in you!

head of house

never married

Lizaveta I hope there is plenty.

Shpigelsky On the subject of 'long life', I must now shock you: between ourselves . . . I'm a bad doctor – no need to disagree.

She stares, inscrutably.

Quite right. Fortunately, most of the locals know no better and I muddle through. My patients remain loyal and my practice is profitable. Have you got that?

Lizaveta nods, writes.

But the fact is I'm a maestro of misdiagnosis and I sometimes prescribe wrongly. On occasions, dangerously. Suffice to say, I'm no stranger to bluff and fervent prayer.

Please be assured that were you – as my wife – to fall ill, I wouldn't dream of treating you myself.

Lizaveta I am relieved to hear it. Please return to your circumstances. Perhaps you could tell me something of your household?

Shpigelsky Well, I must confess it's in chaos; the male servants are rude, the maids are sullen and the cook is a poisoner. You would need to purge this Augean stable. I daresay a blast of your beady disapproval would be a start.

She looks at him disapprovingly.

That's it!

Lizaveta Onwards to your character.

Shpigelsky *Yes* . . . I suspect you've formed an opinion of me over the years? Cheerful and humorous? A luminous fellow?

Lizaveta I've often thought of you as 'vivid'.

Shpigelsky Hmm. Good – I think. But what I must tell you now will stun you: I have the heart of a hard pea. I'm not sweet-natured nor sociable. I'm a hater. For example: I despise Natalya Petrovna. I detest her taste, her snobbery . . .

Lizaveta Her dubious morals . . .

Shpigelsky But you'd never know it from my dealings with her! She thinks I adore her! So you see, I'm *deceptive*. A ruthless social chameleon who plays to win. Yes, I lark about to amuse the gentry but I won't tolerate their ridicule. They fear me, they know I *bite*. There's a rather famous story people tell about me, well, I suppose you know it.

Lizaveta No.

Shpigelsky Really? It's something of a legend. Are you sure?

Lizaveta Yes.

Shpigelsky *Well* . . . I was attending a grand dinner up at the estate west of Bolshintsov's. This was . . . ooh . . . seventeen years ago. At the dining table, a certain young gentleman – supposed gentleman – he placed a radish in my hair.

Lizaveta turns away, concealing her amusement.

I don't know how long that radish sat there. But long enough to provoke a ripple of murmured amusement from my fellow diners. Once I became aware of it can you guess what I did?

Lizaveta Did you remove the offending vegetable?

Shpigelsky Yes, I did. And then, I challenged the man to a duel.

Lizaveta turns to him, intrigued.

The table fell silent. The man froze with terror. Forty, fifty people at that dinner – rapt. The tension. My pitiless stare. His dread. Finally, the host made him apologise. It was a *sensation*!

Lizaveta Would you have gone through with it?

Shpigelsky Oh yes. Though I must confess I knew he wouldn't fight, he was a known coward. *Thus* my character. Any questions?

Lizaveta None that are pressing.

Shpigelsky Now. (*Consults notes.*) Nearly there! 'Regarding the life we might share.' The following is non-negotiable: I like to be served and catered for – but silently, without fuss. I detest chatter and sudden noise. When at

61

home I tend to be morose. I don't know why. Nor do I *want* to know. My inner self is darkly shrouded and will remain so. In short, I won't change. But as long as you try to please me – and don't weep in my presence – I sense that with my steady income and your modest savings we two could live quite amiably beneath one roof. What do you say?

He pockets his notes.

Lizaveta I think the customary procedure in a proposal of marriage is for the gentleman to trumpet his achievements and then lay out a plan for future contentment. You have adopted a rather different approach; you have, as it were, exposed your undergarments and invited me to admire the stains. Why?

Shpigelsky Because I don't want to deceive the woman I marry! I want to live honourably. To live with you in *truth*. Aren't most marriages a mutual conspiracy of grim and silent disappointment? 'Oh, you're *this*. I thought you were *that*.' No. I have chosen to stand before you as the naked beast. My flaws and foibles displayed for your judgement *prior* to the event. I know I seem perverse but one day I'll tell you the story of my life. You might be surprised I survived it at all. People who have never known poverty simply cannot understand it. Hunger puts a demon in the soul. *Rage*. I fight it every day. You see?

Lizaveta nods, quietly moved by him.

Lizaveta Doctor. We have conversed, on occasion, for many years. But you have never shown any interest in me. Why today, why have you pounced?

Shpigelsky Oh . . . call it summer madness.

Lizaveta (*crossly*) I see. You have the sunstroke.

Shpigelsky Forgive me, I was flippant before a truth!

I never spoke before because . . . I didn't have the
words. I sensed you'd scorn me. But my tutelage of
Bolshintsov . . . my fear of death . . . the way you said
'clothing' yesterday . . . the deep and lonely blue of your
eyes this morning . . . these true and simple things have
inspired me.

I've watched you for years. I think you're marvellous.
 I've never loved anyone. I think I could love you.

Lizaveta turns away, flattered, embarrassed.

May I?

She quickly offers her hand. He kisses it. She me l/s?

Please take as long as you need to make your decision.

Lizaveta I shall tell you in four hours.

Shpigelsky Oh. That could mean – anything. One final
grace note: *snuff* – the taking of. I'd rather you didn't.

Lizaveta (*snaps*) Doctor! You ask too much! You have
made a proposal, an ostentatiously long one. But not
without charm. I will now go and think about it and I will
consider its implications for my life and future happiness.
But I shall tell you now that alcohol, music and snuff are
essential for my well-being. On these three phenomena
I will not yield!

Shpigelsky bows, makes a gesture: 'understood'.

Shpigelsky Perhaps another turn in the garden?

Lizaveta As you wish.

Shpigelsky May I sing to you?

Lizaveta I'd rather you didn't. People might see.

Shpigelsky Oh, dear Lizaveta, has no one ever sung for
you?

Lizaveta (*softly*) No.

Shpigelsky I have an atrocious voice but it might tickle you.

Lizaveta nods her consent. Shpigelsky clears his throat and then sings to her in Russian. His voice is strong. They exit together, Shpigelsky still in song.

The iron door opens. Katya emerges from the storeroom.
She straightens her dress. Wipes her brow with a sleeve.
She looks slightly dishevelled. Neatens herself.
Schaaf strides in from the direction of the house.

Schaaf Belyaev?

Katya shakes her head.

Not seen?

Katya I think he's with Kolya.

He stares at her. Then marches to the iron door and flings it open.

Schaaf Magic.

Belyaev emerges from the storeroom. Katya starts to leave.
Their embarrassment is immense.

No, Miss Katerina, do stay! (*To Belyaev.*) Aleksey. All the house is talking, 'Poor Vera loves him, he loves her back, he loves her not, he's leaving, he stays.' As you know, I do not care who or what you love or do not. What I care is I recommend you for this posting. My reputation is joined with yours. I like this house very much. I like my position. I like the people. I want to remain. I want to die here. It's my *life*! Be careful of everyone. Behave. Be discreet. The both of you. *Yes?*

Belyaev (*nods*) My apologies.

A warm moment between them. Schaaf exits. Belyaev and Katya look at each other, slight smile.

Katya Why did he leave Moscow?

Belyaev A scandal. An affair with someone at the University.

Katya I think he loves you.

Belyaev Have you been here before? In there?

Katya It's the place of assignation. All the country estates have one. Some have many.

Belyaev Well, I'm from the city.

Pause.

Katya *Are* you leaving?

Belyaev I hope not. It's precarious.

Katya looks mournful.

Katya I should go and get Miss Vera.

Belyaev Oh, not yet. Look what I found . . .

He takes a large plum from his pocket.

I might never see you again . . .

He hands her the plum. Katya stares at him. He nods. She eats the plum. Slowly. Eyes fixed on him. Belyaev watches. Eyes fixed on her. Finally, she wipes her mouth with her sleeve. They kiss, then part.

Katya Keep the stone.

She exits. Belyaev takes the stone from his mouth.

Belyaev In a hundred years . . . this world and its ways will be ash.

How we lived. And loved. And longed for the future . . .
Who will remember us?

Bolshintsov (*entering*) Where is everyone?! The house is *empty*. It seems they've all dispersed or fled. I've been alone for two hours!

Belyaev You might find the doctor in the garden.

Bolshintsov Have you seen Miss Vera?

Belyaev No.

Bolshintsov She's an elusive lady.
Isn't it odd? Life can feel completely unbearable late at night and then seem perfectly tolerable after a good breakfast.
Might I ask you for some advice?

Belyaev nods.

What does a young man like you say to someone like Miss Vera?

Katya and Vera enter. Bolshintsov gazes at Vera.

Bolshintsov (*bows*) Miss Vera. Good afternoon.

Belyaev (*to Katya*) I think the doctor might be in the garden.

Katya (*to Bolshintsov*) Sir, shall we look for him?

Before he can speak she leads Bolshintsov off. Vera faces Belyaev.

Vera Last night. You spoke to Natalya Petrovna.

Belyaev Yes.

Vera What about?

Belyaev . . . It was a private conversation.

Vera Did she betray my confidence?
Did she tell you I love you? Did she?

Belyaev Yes.

Vera It's not true.

Belyaev looks confused.

Not as she'd have told it. She doesn't know love. Not
love that seeks nothing in return. Not love that is true
and freely given.
How did you respond?

Belyaev I expressed my sincere feelings for you.

Vera I'm not a child. Spare me your 'sincere feelings'.

Belyaev I told her that I have a great fondness for you
and that I adore your company.

Pause.

Vera But you don't love me.
Were you lying?
To protect our secrecy?

Pause.

Belyaev No.

Vera breaks down.

Vera (*softly*) It makes no sense . . .

Belyaev looks at her with compassion.

Belyaev If I could do anything to help you.

Vera But you can . . . You could love me . . . YOU
COULD LOVE ME!! YOU COULD LOVE ME!! Why
don't you do that?

Belyaev And if I did?

She gestures tersely, 'I don't know.'

Where would we *go*, what would we *do*? I exist like a student; I'm poor, I'm lost, I'm *nothing*! I'm no use to you!

Vera I don't need you to *be* something, I need you to want me.

Belyaev Living in one room when you can live in a house like this? With land and servants and numerous rooms?

Vera What use are rooms?

Belyaev One day you'll know.

He looks at her, guiltily.

I'm sorry if I led you to believe.

Vera (*shakes her head*) I led myself.

Pause.

Belyaev I know I'll regret this. You're wonderful.

Vera Yes. I am.

She thinks. Suddenly chasing a new thought . . .

Your talk with my betrayer, how did it conclude?

Belyaev Natalya Petrovna will give me her decision today. I think I'll be leaving.

Vera What did she say, when you told her my love was unrequited?

Belyaev I don't remember.

Vera Yes – she was *relieved*! She teases it out of me – and then she speaks with you – *yes*!

Natalya appears at the door from the house.

Don't you see?!

Natalya comes in. Vera fixes her.

(*Raging.*) She was going to marry me off! She wants rid of me! She's in love with you! She wants you for herself! I HATE YOU! *Your love, goes fast, lots of emotion* 5

Vera flies at Natalya, tries to hit her, but Belyaev holds her back.

Vera is savage – she lashes out at Belyaev.

Now you touch me! You protect *her* – why not *me*?!

She breaks free. Snarls at Belyaev with contempt.

Don't you understand? *I'm* the girl! I'm the girl, you *idiot*! IT WAS ME! I WROTE THE POETRY!

She exits. Belyaev makes to go after her.

Natalya Don't!

He turns back. Natalya looks away, ashamed.

She's right. I've wronged her.
I've abused her trust and there is no excuse.
And she's right that I'm in love with you.

Belyaev stares, in shock.

I've loved you from the day you arrived.
And now, I must ask you to leave.
We'll arrange your transport after lunch. I hope that three months' wages will be acceptable to you?

Belyaev vaguely nods.

We are all most grateful for the life and spirit you have brought to this house.

She looks at him now. Holds back her tears.

I imagine that now you know my feelings . . . you would not want to stay here. And I'm sorry to have told you and to have embarrassed you.

You're mortified.
I shouldn't have told you.
I've told you because I love you.
I won't see you again.
I won't know you.
But I wanted you to know that you are loved.
Loved by a foolish woman who lacks the grace and dignity to control herself.
When you leave . . . please don't feel obligated to say goodbye. I won't consider it an impoliteness.
I would appreciate it if you could speak to Kolya. He'll . . . you can imagine. And in time, if you could bring yourself to write to him . . .?

Belyaev nods. Tries to speak. Can't.

Oh, please say something.

He approaches. Takes her hand, kisses it, tenderly.
Natalya almost faints.

Belyaev (*softly*) Don't make me leave.

Natalya There's no other way.

Belyaev I return your love.

Natalya You don't have to lie.

Belyaev Yesterday. We both knew. You know I love you.

Natalya shakes her head.

Natalya Whether you do or don't, it's impossible. But . . . do you?

Belyaev kisses her, full on the mouth. She responds.
They part. Do it again.

Natalya thinks. Struggles.

No. Pack your bags. *Go.*

Belyaev Come with me. Run away with me. Now!

Natalya I can't.

Belyaev Yes you can!

Natalya I can't!

Belyaev Why?

Natalya Kolya.

Belyaev We'll take him with us!

Natalya No. It's *wrong*.

Belyaev But do it. Live as you long to. *Live!*

Pause.

Natalya I can't.

Belyaev Why not?

Natalya I don't have the courage.

Belyaev goes to kiss her again. She embraces him just as Rakitin enters. They part. Rakitin stares.

Rakitin Your husband is looking for you.

Rakitin breathes in, trying to control himself.

Has a decision been made?

Natalya Concerning?

Rakitin The general arrangements. I can't keep up.

Natalya Yes. We've spoken. And reached an agreement.

She turns to Belyaev.

The tutor will stay. For as long as he wants.

Belyaev is stunned.

We're pleased to have resolved this matter.

Belyaev bows and exits. Rakitin nods to the iron door.

Rakitin Did you take him in there?

Natalya No.

Rakitin Oh. Why not?

Natalya You came in.

Rakitin So sorry.

Natalya (*casually*) I forgive you.

  Pause.

  Rakitin goes to the iron door. Almost flinches before it.

Rakitin Remember?

Natalya Of course.

Rakitin Think about it?

Natalya Never.

  Rakitin stands at the threshold.

Rakitin You could slip in here after lunch.

Natalya I hadn't thought of that.

Rakitin Yes. When everyone's having a snooze.

Natalya Good idea.

Rakitin I could keep watch.

Natalya Oh, we wouldn't want to put you out.

Rakitin Really, no trouble at all. And then I'll be gone.
  Natasha. I have to know. Why don't you love me?

  Arkady comes in. Stares at them. Feels their tension.

Arkady (*to Rakitin*) Please stop avoiding me.

Rakitin There's nothing to hide, my friend.

Arkady Why does that worry me?

Realising his marriage is now hopeless, why try to fix it?

Rakitin We'll have that talk, straight after lunch. My word on it.

Arkady I was just thinking about this place. We're wasting its potential. If we take this wall out, open it through to the old storeroom – no one uses it – if we open it up ... if we open it ... we could ... Who cares. Natasha?

> *He offers his arm, Natalya takes it. They exit.*
> *Rakitin rests his forehead against the iron door.*
> *Shpigelsky and Bolshintsov appear.*

Shpigelsky The noble Rakitin!

Rakitin My God, still *here*.

Shpigelsky Have you spoken to the lady of the house? To advance our cause?

Bolshintsov Leave him alone, can't you see he's upset?

> *Rakitin looks at Bolshintsov with pity and contempt.*

Rakitin At lunch; be bold, seize it, *twinkle*.

Bolshintsov I should charm Miss Vera with a smile?

Rakitin Yes. Be sweet, be simple. I have come to realise that all other methods of seduction are a waste of time.

Shpigelsky (*to Rakitin*) Sound advice from the master.

Rakitin Doctor. You make me sick.

> *Rakitin exits. Shpigelsky spots his handkerchief left on the crate, mops his brow with it, then puts it in his pocket and exits with Bolshintsov.*

> *Empty stage. The iron door.*

Handwritten at top:
Discovery: Rakitin loves Natasha. Our marriage is
(subtext) officially over...
They love each other.

Five

The drawing room. Same day. Late afternoon.

Anna stands. Arkady stands. Matvey waits.

Handwritten left margin: Still huffy, hopeless

Arkady Resolution. (*To Matvey.*) Go to the weir and
stand them down. All of them.

Matvey Yes, sir.

Arkady If they want a reason tell them to look in a
mirror. *Handwritten: → I'm the failure, my reflection*
     What's wrong?

Matvey It's private, sir.

Handwritten left margin: 'Get out of here' 3 days ago

Arkady Fine. Off you go.

Matvey Katya has ended our relationship. She says she
wants 'passion'. She says that what she had with me was a
feeble compromise. Her words. I am a feeble compromise.

Arkady I'm sorry to hear it.

Matvey Thank you, sir.

He exits.

Anna Arkasha . . . my dear boy . . .

Arkady Mama, please don't.

Anna Go and talk to Rakitin!

Arkady I don't know where he is. *Handwritten: I really don't, so it works as a good excuse.*

Anna He's in the billiard room.

Arkady He *promised* he'd come and see me. What's he
doing in there?

Anna He's playing billiards.

Arkady With who?

Anna The professor, the doctor and our unfortunate neighbour.

Arkady What a loathsome gathering, what a disgusting cabal of appalling men. *to myself*

Anna He's your closest friend. Since you were children.

Arkady And he's insulting me!

Anna So tell him! What else can you do?

Arkady I can do nothing. I like 'nothing'. I know what it is.

Ignore w/ newspaper

Anna Go and speak to him.

Arkady No!

Anna Such cowardice. *← ooh.*

Arkady Avoidance has its virtues. It requires great discipline to look away.

Anna There is nothing more painful than watching your child suffer.

Arkady I'm not a child.

Anna Prove it! Talk to him. And once you've managed that, talk to your son.

Arkady flinches.

Why won't you be with Kolya?
    He's your heir. This is *his*.
    He needs you.
    Make him a bow and arrow.

Arkady He has one.

Handwritten top: I'm becoming my father. I am horrified at that.

Anna Father him! *Big ach.*

Arkady looks away, enraged.

Why won't you engage with anyone? *+ my father.*

Arkady Because ... *Mother* ... *You're not* I am truly desolate.
  And I don't want to inflict myself on those who I love.

  Pause. *Genuine*

Anna For all her qualities, you married a restless woman.
You've always known. You found her in the street and
fell in love. Now deal with the consequences.

  She exits. *Catharsis? to the just openness*

Arkady Why do the people who most care for you insist
on poking their fingers in your deepest wounds?

  He composes himself. Anna returns with Rakitin.

Anna Your friend.

  Anna exits.

Arkady Billiards. *Huffing*

Rakitin I know.

Arkady You don't even play.

Rakitin I know.

Arkady You hate billiards.

Rakitin I was keeping score for them.

  Pause.

Arkady Will you tell me the truth?

Rakitin Yes.

  Pause.

Arkady Well?

Rakitin Sorry, I thought you were going to ask me some questions.

Pause.

Arkady Well?

Rakitin You're not going to ask any questions?

Arkady No! I'm assuming you're going to explain or confess or apologise! Oh, shall we forget it?

Rakitin I love her.

Pause.

Arkady Well, of course you do. She's magnificent. Extraordinary. Impossible.

Rakitin I love her.

Pause.

Arkady For how long?

Rakitin Long.

Pause.

Arkady Why didn't you say?

Rakitin I love both of you. What could I say?

Arkady But you should have . . .

Rakitin What?

Arkady Said something!

Rakitin To what end?

Pause.

Arkady Oh. She returns your love.

Rakitin No. She occasionally indulges mine. She's never loved me.

77

She endures me.
I amuse her.
I used to.
That's all it is.

Pause.

[handwritten: True pity]

Arkady Oh, my poor fellow. All these years . . . ? Oh, my friend.

She should've chosen you. You're far better suited. What madness propelled her in my direction? I mean, I'm grateful it did. But . . .
[handwritten: genuine]
Is this why she's been so agitated?

Rakitin Yes.

Arkady Have your conversations come to an end?

Rakitin They have.

Arkady She's been protecting me while the two of you resolved this?

Rakitin Yes.

Arkady . . . Because she still cares for me?

Rakitin Yes.

Pause.

[handwritten: know she would have an affair one day]

Arkady I've always feared she never loved me. I feared she wanted this . . . (*Gestures to room and outside.*) Or something . . . way beyond me. I'm a poor husband. I'm not good at love. *[handwritten: actual confession]*

Rakitin Yes you are. And she . . . she loves you. And now I must go. *[handwritten: "Wait, permanently??"]*

Arkady clasps Rakitin to him.

Arkady You can't leave!

Rakitin I have to.

[handwritten left margin: Should I trust him? Yes, b/c I want + need a friend.]

[handwritten bottom: Most introspective he's ever been.]

78

Arkady But you'll come back?

Rakitin No.

Arkady But we *need* you here! I . . . I can't fathom her!

I can't figure her out.

Rakitin I'm saying goodbye.

Arkady *Please.* I'll have no one to talk to.

Rakitin Talk to Belyaev. He's interesting.

Arkady No, he's not.

Rakitin Watch him.

Arkady shakes hands with Rakitin then hugs him.

Arkady I won't say goodbye. I don't accept it. I'm going to the barn to kick someone.

He exits. Rakitin stands, mournfully.
Belyaev enters. He hands Rakitin his magazine.

Belyaev Sir, your *Contemporary*. Thank you.

Rakitin Oh, keep it.

Belyaev I couldn't possibly.

Rakitin Yes you could.

Rakitin offers the magazine – forces it – until Belyaev takes it.

New coat?

Belyaev No.

Rakitin What a lovely flower. What a splendid thing to see in a young man's buttonhole.

Belyaev makes to remove the flower from his buttonhole.

Belyaev Then you must have it.

Rakitin Oh, I couldn't possibly.

I'm leaving. I think you should come with me.
Bolshintsov has room in his carriage. He'll take us into
town. We'll be in Moscow next week.

Belyaev Leaving? I'm sorry to hear it.

Rakitin There's no need! It's an empty room!

Belyaev Why are you leaving?

Rakitin Because my beloved friend – your employer –
suspects that I'm in love with his wife. And so, to protect
her *honour* – which is sacred – I must leave. Of course,
his suspicions are groundless. The notion that *I* threaten
his marriage is comical. But a decent man must be
prepared to sacrifice his pleasure for the greater good.
It's what defines us. Were you in my position you'd do
the same.

Belyaev But I'm not.

Rakitin Well, that's disappointing. I've misread you.
I took you for a young gentleman – what with your floral
display.

Belyaev I'm engaged here, by contract. I intend to
honour it.

Rakitin Aren't you sly? Listen – *child* – Natalya Petrovna
is an innocent. Despite her sophistication, she's *innocent*.
If you have any humanity you'll end this now! You'll
spare her the pain you inflict wherever you go!

Belyaev You know nothing of my life!

Rakitin (*raging*) I know it *all*! I've *lived* it! You think
love is a blessing?! Oh, you can't wait to succumb to it,
to know all its terrible intensity. You dream of soft little
hands – don't you? Their tender solicitude as they tear
your heart to pieces. Wait! You will know the hatred

which burns love out. And you will remember *me* – look –
as a sick man longs for health – you will remember my
dead eyes and broken heart and you will know humiliation.
You'll yearn to be an idiot – a holy fool – a eunuch!
You'll envy rough men who brawl in the street, envy the
honesty of their bloody wounds when yours are hidden –
you'll envy animals and trees and rivers and rocks!
Because – wait – you will know what it is to be enslaved –
to dream in flickering glimpses of legs and eyes and
mouth – to remember each day <u>one kiss of seven years</u>
ago. Did she love me? Yes! That *moment* she did! How
did I lose her? Oh the teeth and the breath and her hands –
what she whispered – did she – *yes* – she murmured
something *so* important – aaaggghhh – forgotten it!
You'll hate yourself – hate women – hate life – hate your
desperate heart for needing love – *hear* me: never love
nor *be* loved – only then are you safe! You don't believe
me! But my God, you *will*!

Pause.

Belyaev Thank you for a most revealing lecture.

Rakitin I was babbling. Do excuse me.

*He turns away in shame. Can't stop his tears. He's
shaking. And now Rakitin faces Belyaev, weeping
openly.*

I would've died for her – and now I *have*!

*Natalya and Vera enter from the garden.
     A silence. Rakitin is shaking. No one can speak.*

I must go and pack.

*He bows to all and exits. Vera sits. Natalya and
Belyaev remain standing. Eventually . . .*

Natalya We were in the garden . . .

81

Belyaev Yes. I was thinking of going for a walk.

Natalya Perhaps we could accompany you . . .

Vera My God! Is this how it's going to be? Is this IT?

Natalya can only look at Belyaev.
Belyaev thinks. Looks between the two women.
Makes his decision.

Belyaev I need to give this back to him.

He waves the magazine, stares at Natalya a moment,
then exits.
Natalya kneels before Vera.

Natalya I've been apologising all afternoon! I don't expect
to be forgiven, but try to understand!

Vera (*furiously*) Oh, I see it all! He *loves* you. So easy to
say sorry when you're loved! I'm just a little problem to
be dealt with before you can wallow in happiness. I'll
never forgive you!

Natalya You're seventeen. I'm considerably older. But
just as you have found first love, so have I!

Vera What?! You're a flirt, a tease! Desperate to be
desired and so easily won!

Natalya slaps her. Once.

There. Even your gestures are cheap!

Natalya You think you *know*, child? You don't, you
can't. You won't know what it is to waste your life until
you've done it. To be old, to lose what beauty you had.
And then: to find love! To know it at last and feel its
force. Forgive me this joy that fills me! You're in pain and
I'm sorry – but you don't understand – I hope you never
do. We'll finish this when your blood is cooler.

She leaves the room. Vera thinks a moment.

Vera Katya.

Katya enters.

Please could you ask the doctor to come in?

Katya Are you unwell, miss?

Vera Yes.

Katya Can I get you anything?

Vera *Yes*, the doctor.

Katya exits.

I have *worth*. Now let them see.

Shpigelsky enters. Hurries to Vera.

Shpigelsky What is it?

He touches her forehead.

Such life in you! But you take it too seriously, dear girl.
   We're passing through on the breeze. Be *light* . . .

Vera Good Doctor. Is Bolshintsov kind?

Shpigelsky Yes. He really is.

Vera He's not bad-tempered? Or aggressive?

Shpigelsky No! He's not a man, he's a dove.

Vera Tell him I'll marry him. Tell him now.

Shpigelsky Are you certain?

Vera Yes but it must be quick – *tomorrow*. Can it be
done?

Shpigelsky Of course! But why don't you tell him
yourself – he's in the billiard room!

Vera (*furiously*) I want to marry him, I don't want to *see*
him!

Shpigelsky He'll be so happy!

Vera Please make the arrangements.

Shpigelsky Congratulations!

Vera And don't tell anyone. Hurry!

She makes an impatient, frustrated gesture.

Shpigelsky I will gallop to him now!

He makes for the door. Shpigelsky exits as Belyaev enters.

Out the way!

Belyaev faces Vera.

Belyaev I know the damage I've done.

Vera Do you?

Belyaev I won't do more.
I'm leaving. This moment. I'm going to walk. The carriage will pick me up on the road. I'm not meant for rich ladies. I belong in Moscow. Our country is dying. I have work to do. Please will you give her this?

He hands Vera a note. She reads it.

Vera It's one word. You're really not a writer.

Belyaev I didn't say I was.

Vera Why *her*?

Belyaev It wasn't her. Or if it was, the moment it was spoken . . . it ceased to be.

Vera Not for her. She'll be devastated. You've killed her.
Next time you say the words: mean them.
Have you told Kolya you're going?

Belyaev Yes. He's very upset.
But you'll love him so much better than I can.

Belyaev → father figure
Arkady → Money & home
Rakitin → Emotional support / Sexual attention

84

She stares at him.

Vera Yesterday we made a kite.

Belyaev bows, exits. Lizaveta comes in.

Lizaveta Have you seen the doctor?

Vera Billiard room.

Lizaveta Ah. I just heard some bellowing from in there. I dared not enter the cave. Is he with that dreadful Bolshintsov?

Vera Yes.

Shpigelsky comes in, beaming.

Shpigelsky (*to Vera*) He's exploded! BOOM!

He laughs, then sees Lizaveta.

Two miraculous beings in one room! (*To heaven.*) Take me now!

Lizaveta May we speak privately?

Shpigelsky No need, Verochka and I share many secrets. Speak, good lady!

Lizaveta If you insist . . .?

Shpigelsky I do. (*To Vera, almost winking.*) And with good reason! Wait for this . . .

Lizaveta I'm afraid I must decline your generous proposal.

Pause.

Shpigelsky Proposal?

Lizaveta The one you made this morning.

Shpigelsky . . . Decline?

Lizaveta Yes.

Shpigelsky It wasn't exactly a proposal, more . . . the offer of an arrangement.

Lizaveta Whatever it was, I don't want it.

Shpigelsky May I ask why?

Lizaveta I can live with my unhappiness. I don't want to live with yours.

Pause.

Shpigelsky Is that *it*?

Lizaveta Yes.

Shpigelsky It's not about the snuff?

Lizaveta No.

Pause.

Shpigelsky Well I . . . I'm very sad. Are you sure?

Lizaveta Quite.

Shpigelsky You'd rather be alone than . . . Do excuse me.

Shpigelsky takes out his handkerchief, exits.
    Lizaveta exhales with relief. Vera catches her eye, smiles.
    Natalya comes in from the garden.

Natalya Kolya's in tears. He's sobbing in the garden.

Lizaveta I'll go.

She hurries out to the garden.

Natalya He's inconsolable. His kite's all broken. But he says that's not the reason. (*To Vera.*) He says you'll know.

Vera faces Natalya.

Vera Sit down.

Natalya Why?

Natalya remains standing. Vera hands her the note.
Natalya reads it.

When?

Vera A few minutes ago.

Natalya Where is he?

Vera Walking away.

Natalya starts to move.

Don't. He's gone. He's left you. Don't make a scene.

Natalya What did he say?

Vera He said that once the words were spoken, the
feeling was dead.

Pause.

Natalya He's gone.
He fled from me.
He never loved me.
It was all for nothing.   *A beat of Vera staring*

She collapses. Curls up. Broken. Vera watches a while
as Natalya convulses in pain. Arkady comes in, sees
Natalya.

Arkady Get the doctor!   *fear for my love*

Vera rushes out. Arkady holds Natalya. She pushes
him away, he clings to her.
                                    Calm reassurance
Darling. Natasha. I know. I know.   *to calm Nat, but w/ urgency)*
  But he told me everything – and we're still the best of
friends.   *we left on best of terms*
  He's leaving but we'll survive.
  How we were. Remember?

Natalya sobs in his arms. He holds her.

I know = I know you might
have regrets about leaving of us,
but I forgive you.

87

Arkady Remember how we loved each other?

[handwritten: Wants so much to begin love again both]

[handwritten: We used to be strong in love years ago, but now is less]

Shpigelsky hurries in, followed by Schaaf, Bolshintsov and Rakitin.
    Katya appears with a glass of water. Anna, Matvey and Vera watch from the door. Lizaveta comes in from the garden.

Shpigelsky Here, dear lady. Take these.

He gives Natalya some pills. Katya hovers with the glass.

Natalya No!

Shpigelsky I think you should.

Natalya I DON'T WANT TO!

Shpigelsky Please, dear lady.

Natalya NO!

Arkady (*sternly*) Natasha. Take them! *[handwritten: Lifting fast]*

Natalya takes the pills. Gulps the water.

(*To Rakitin.*) But she knew you were going last night. Why the distress? *[handwritten: why now + not last night??]*

Rakitin I couldn't tell you.

Shpigelsky and Arkady help Natalya to her feet.

Shpigelsky A little rest. She must rest. Make way, please.

He helps Natalya to the door. She stops. Turns.

Natalya I'm sorry. I wish I could explain. I wish it were different. All of it.
    You are such splendid people.
    How well you conduct yourselves.
    I'm sorry I'm so disappointing.

He loved the house. That's all.

Rakitin catches her eye.

Oh. Goodbye.
I'm so ashamed.
And so . . .
So stupid.

She exits, followed by Katya, Arkady and Shpigelsky.

Rakitin After twenty years of obsession: 'Oh. Goodbye.'
It's bracing, really.

He picks up Belyaev's note, left on the floor.

Lizaveta (*to Matvey*) I can't find Kolya. He might be at
the lake.

Matvey nods, exits.

Rakitin Well. Goodbye everyone!

*Rakitin says his goodbyes to Anna, Lizaveta and
Schaaf.*
Meanwhile, Bolshintsov sidles up to Vera.

Bolshintsov Miss Vera. Will I see you tomorrow?

Vera Yes. And you may call me Verochka.

She offers her hand, he presses it.

Bolshintsov I will be honoured. Thank you.

*She stares at him. He bows to her and exits. Vera
shudders.*
Now Rakitin approaches Vera and hugs her.

Rakitin I'll miss you.

Vera When you see Belyaev tell him . . . tell him . . .
I wish him good luck. You're to say it affectionately.

Rakitin If I must.

He hugs her again.

Be good. Be brave.

Vera Write to me.

Rakitin nods, then takes one last look at the room.

Rakitin Goodbye!

Anna We must see you off. Verochka?

*Rakitin exits, followed by Anna, Lizaveta and Vera.
Schaaf is alone for a while.
Kolya comes in from the garden with his bow and arrow.
He points it at Schaaf who slowly raises his hands.
Kolya stares at him, the bow drawn, tense.*

Schaaf Kolya. Don't kill me.

Kolya Why not?

Schaaf Because I am friend not foe.

Kolya slowly lowers the weapon.

Kolya I want to cry.

Schaaf goes to him.

Schaaf You have a cry. Don't be ashamed.

Kolya falls into his arms, sobs.

Very good. There. There it is.
Remember this.
Because one day you will want to cry but you won't
know how.
Now. Time for lesson.

Kolya nods, sadly.

Except today I teach you . . . here.

*Schaaf pulls out a chair at the card table and sits
down.
Schaaf sits opposite Kolya and starts to shuffle –
beautifully, brilliantly.*

Kolya is amused by this. Schaaf deals to Kolya and himself.

Now. Look at your cards.

Kolya does so, a touch clumsily, exposing some cards. Schaaf makes a gesture.

Conceal!
Don't show your hand.
Never.
Now . . .
How many hearts do you have?

Kolya counts them.

Kolya Three.

Schaaf Good. Very good. You will need them.

They start to play.

3 men → 3 hearts
3 potential father figures

Corbett stage: Give emotions out to the
audience, not the floor. Breathiness
w/ secrets, not softer. Keep released
volume. Don't indulge, no unneccesary
space in between thoughts/ Speaking too
quickly & pushed. No compensation for
lack of stakes, breathe it in instead!
* Take what we've done & let it go.

Why does someone new in the room make us
more self-conscious? It's a bit weird.

Don't act, just be. Exist in the space

Include the audience in your discoveries.
Avoid downward inflection at the end
of sentences.

Rebecca voice notes: 🎵

Relish in the elegant vocabulary. Journey in the
sentence

Don't get stuck in a memorized vocal cadence.
Try new things to make the moment fresh.

After many rehearsals: Don't get trapped in
speaking words without thinking them. Always
think in character.

Rubikin & I's scene:
    Care about him, care about Natalya,
    Care about myself more. These struggle
    VS. the hurt & fear that I feel
    about losing my marriage & best friend.
    - Want to be mad at him, but I can't

Colin notes:
Don't push - change volume, pitch, duration
    to emphasize. Lower= higher pitch, higher=
    must change pitch

Rebecca voice notes:

Talk straighter, through your back and out
to the back row.
Don't drop arms so much
Turn out - don't profile too much.

The stage is a playground. Play - explore within
a structure. Know where you need to be; but
your journey can be free & in the moment.

Costume notes:
Add hat to Act 2
Remove jacket w/ Raditin scene

Wednesday, June 30ᵗʰ: 1 day until performance
Allow the world to be more lucrative so that
my mind is in the moment. Even a performance
is free.
Our related run today is exactly how the
performance should be. It should feel
loose. Listen to some meditation tracks or
something funny before a show to lighten
up.

Thursday, July 1ˢᵗ: Opening night!

Exit SL or SR Act 2
keep it bold, keep it confident, keep it
         focused.

Forgetting how you did s/t, so that its fresh
the next run / performance.

Spend a few minutes preparing backstage.

Saterday: Matinee

We warmed-up hard and it was a bit exhausting.
First half dragged, low-energy. We need to be
more at the forefront for the second half.

10% : Actor Brain
90% : In the world